# Life on the Road

*Around the World on Four Wheels*

gestalten

# *Itinerary*

*Introduction*

4

Kindness and Resilience on the Road through
the Balkans and the Middle East

10

Nomadic Life and Nature's Infinite Variety in the Vastness
of Central Asia, Russia, and Mongolia

48

Eastbound Escapades in South Korea and Japan

88

A Multi-Stage Sojourn among the Dense Rainforests
of Borneo and Indonesia

114

A Year Traversing the Many Expanses of Mainland
Australia and Tasmania

144

Endless Stories across Canada, the USA, and Mexico

192

*Epilogue*

255

# Circumnavigation by Road

Wild landscapes, changing seasons, and indelible encounters on the adventure of a lifetime

---

Our journey started in Austria, our home country. In a nearly 50-year-old Mercedes-Benz truck, a former border-patrol vehicle that we bought in 2014 and dubbed "Akela," we—Leander, Maria, and Lennox—began a trip that would see us circumnavigating the globe over a period of seven years. Heading east through the Balkan states, we crossed Turkey and Iran—once over the Caspian Sea we explored Kazakhstan. We then ventured along the ancient Silk Road and the Pamir Highway—the second-highest mountain pass in the world—into Russia and Mongolia. We traversed Siberia in the freezing cold, then shipped Akela by ferry to South Korea; once in East Asia, we also explored Japan and Indonesia. We then boarded a freighter to Australia, a country we circled over the course of a year. Crossing the ocean by boat again to Los Angeles, we drove up to Canada, back through the U.S. and Mexico, and eventually came back to Europe after a full circumnavigation of the globe.

Our goal, initially, was simply to reach New Zealand by land and, when necessary, boat. We had planned a full year for the venture, but due to strict entry regulations regarding vehicles and various bureaucratic hurdles, we never made it. Instead, what was supposed to be a one-year trip turned into a seven-year voyage, a total lifestyle transformation that saw us travel across four continents and 35 countries, covering 81,000 miles (130,000 kilometers) in the process. As we learned repeatedly on our passage through mountains and rainforests, deserts and steppes, sometimes the road you travel can be quite different from the one you planned.

Our life before the trip was in many respects idyllic—we had an adorable young son, a charming home in the country, safe jobs. Still, something kept gnawing at us: a desire to break free from our day-to-day routine, to take off and experience the beauty of the world with our son. One evening, over a glass of wine, the idea emerged: "Why not travel to the other side of the world in our own vehicle?" A dream was born, and an old Mercedes-Benz truck became the symbol of our desire to shake up our predictable lives.

We deliberately chose a sturdy, off-road vehicle to ensure that we could travel off the beaten path in the safest way possible. The conversion phase was challenging, though, as the truck's existing structure was rusted and unusable. Over the next two years, we transformed the old truck into a robust expedition vehicle that met our specifications as a family.

After two years, our mobile home was ready. We gave up our old rental apartment, sold our belongings, and quit our jobs. Downsizing to 129 square feet (12 square meters) brought obvious challenges. With a mere tenth of our former living space, everyday tasks like laundry or cooking had to be reimagined; the texture of our everyday routines and Lennox's schooling needed rethinking. Naturally, the prospect of our sudden freedom brought fears and doubts, but we were determined to explore the world.

Four continents and 35 countries later, an idea first hatched over a glass of wine became a way of life defined by breathtaking landscapes and the extraordinary kindness of the people we met worldwide. Over the course of our long journey, we learned the advantages of living a simple, resource-conscious life—gradually, we discerned the difference between being a traveler and a tourist, between a road-trip vacation and life on the road. In these pages you'll find a record of some of the breathtaking places we visited, places that inspired our continuing awe for planet Earth in all its variety and renewed our desire to protect and preserve its many riches. From waters teeming with manta rays in Indonesia to mist-wreathed clifftop monasteries in Greece, we hope to inspire readers just as we have been.

The journey changed our way of thinking, and it's this new mindset that guides us toward future adventures.

## A Home for the Road

In 2014, Maria and Leander saw an online listing for an old Mercedes-Benz truck, a former military vehicle used to monitor Germany's borders. It seemed like a twist of fate that what had once served to patrol borders was now destined to carry the travelers across them. On first inspection, it was clear the existing living cabin was mostly rust. After much deliberation, the couple detached the old cabin and installed a completely new one onto the frame. Thus began a long process, one that involved countless hours of research and endless budgeting. When one set of questions was answered, a whole new set of questions arose. Finally, the truck—lovingly named "Akela"—was ready to hit the road. The truck's compact, wood-paneled cabin features a double bed (that transitions to a table and seating area); a separate bunk above; a woodstove; steps separating the living areas; solar panels and a boiler; clever storage; and a sink and toilet. In this space measuring only 129 square feet (12 square meters), the family ate, slept, wrote, did laundry and chores, and made meals. It was their home.

INTRODUCTION

"In this space measuring only 129 square feet (12 square meters), the family ate, slept, wrote, did laundry and chores, and made meals. It was their home."

---

The family designed their cabin entirely according to their own ideas, desires, and functional needs, placing special emphasis on natural materials, especially wood. Despite all the coziness, they still enjoyed watching the sunrise from the tent—pictured above, with the breathtaking view of Mount Bromo on Java, Indonesia.

# Kindness and Resilience on the Road through the Balkans and the Middle East

Discovering the hidden treasures of the Balkans in wintertime, plus majestic and dreamlike landscapes in Turkey and Iran

---

In the frosty December of 2016, Leander, Maria, and their four-year-old son Lennox set out on a journey into the unknown. As night fell in their Austrian hometown, the family's converted truck, Akela, roared to life, and they began their first of many night shifts on the road. While Lennox was lulled to sleep by the gentle rocking of the truck, Leander and Maria drove until the early hours of the morning, passing through both Austria and Slovenia.

With the first light of morning, they reached the port city of Zadar in Croatia. The Adriatic Coast, bustling with life in the summer months, now presented itself as quiet and deserted in the winter cool. The gentle sound of the waves accompanied the trio on a stroll along the harbor, the dark-blue sea shimmering all around them. At that moment, time seemed to stand still, and they savored the silence. They had previously only known the Dalmatian Coast during those busy summer months, where they had been forced to share its many idyllic spots with other tourists. Now they drove leisurely along the palm-lined coastal road, passing closed hotels and restaurants, rarely encountering other people. They parked easily at picturesque coves, took long walks on the deserted beaches, and let themselves be soothed to sleep at night by the sounds of the sea.

The journey led them swiftly through Montenegro, Albania, and North Macedonia. The Balkan Mountains shape the landscape of these countries impressively. Steep peaks rise above deep valleys, where dark lakes rest and rivers rush. Winter painted the land in a stark but fascinating light. Even the trees defied the cold season, cloaked in their evergreen garments.

The physical traces of the Yugoslav Wars of the 1990s were unmistakable. The dissolution of former Yugoslavia has left Montenegro, Albania, and North Macedonia indelibly marked by the consequences of the conflict. Destroyed houses and abandoned military facilities—including guard towers and ruined barracks—stand as reminders of the not-so-distant past. The rural populations of these states often lead simple and austere lives, while young people migrate to cities in search of work. Despite these cultural differences, people greeted Leander, Maria, and Lennox with extraordinary kindness and helpfulness.

In North Macedonia, the travelers were unexpectedly met by a blanket of snow, and Akela needed some help to get used to the cold temperatures. From there, they continued to Greece, specifically to the city of Kalabaka, then further to the Peloponnese region. There they found the mystical monasteries of Meteora, perched high on distinctive rock pillars. These centuries-old buildings dominated the landscape with their majestic presence, giving a sense of both architecture and spirituality enduring across time and space.

Near the city of Lamia, the history of Thermopylae, too, started to feel alive. Here one finds not only natural hot springs with healing sulfur baths, but also the site of the legendary battle in 480 BCE between the Spartan leader Leonidas I's Greek alliance and the vastly larger army of the First Persian Empire, led by Xerxes. Although the Greeks lost this unequal battle (the Spartans famously numbered only 300), Leonidas remains a hero—not just in the popular imagination, but also for Lennox, who showed great interest in Greek history and mythology.

From Athens, the family crossed over to Crete, where they were greeted by radiant sunshine and endless beaches. Along the island's northern coast, they drove through gentle grasslands, which, as they ventured south, transformed into high mountain peaks and foothills where goatherds grazed their flocks. Back on the Greek mainland, they headed north to Mount Parnassus, the seat of the ancient Muses, the goddesses of the arts and sciences. This mountain range is not only significant in Greek mythology but also home to an excellent ski resort, and, as enthusiastic skiers, the trio naturally came prepared with the necessary gear. Lennox was excited; he had never been on skis before.

Leaving Greece, the journey took them onwards to the Bosphorus Bridge, which, in addition to connecting different districts in Istanbul, also links Continental

Europe to Asia. In 1973, the iconic suspension bridge was inaugurated, and since then, has stood as a symbol of exchange between the two continents. As the family rolled across the bridge in their truck, the Bosphorus Strait revealed itself, crisscrossed with passing cargo ships. On both sides of the bridge, the breathtaking skyline of Istanbul came into view, with its distinctive blend of historic buildings and mosques and modern skyscrapers. The atmosphere on the bridge was lively and bustling as vehicles came and went.

Their journey then led them far inland, to the surreal landscapes of Cappadocia in Turkey's Central Anatolia Region. Here countless rock formations, known as fairy chimneys, towered high into the sky, the result of centuries of erosion. An underground city stretches beneath the distinctive rocks, with some of the formations housing cave dwellings and churches carved into the tuff stone. This area was once a significant center for various cultures and civilizations, including the Hittites, Persians, Greeks, Romans, Byzantines, and Ottomans. Today, Cappadocia is a popular tourist destination, renowned for its unique landforms, historic sites, and breathtaking hot-air balloon rides over the scenery. It was thrilling for the family to be awakened early in the morning by the sounds of hot-air balloons drifting overhead.

On their way eastward into Iran, the trio passed through the cities of Erzincan and Erzurum. The weather was in transition, no longer winter but not yet summer. Some days, the sun shone from a cloudless, blue sky, while on others, snow and icy temperatures prevailed, especially in the higher elevations. Gradually, gently rolling hills gave way to vast plains and agricultural fields, while further east, the land became increasingly mountainous. Standing at 16,854 feet (5,137 meters), Greater Ararat, the highest peak in Turkey, soon dominates the vista.

In Turkey, the Akela crew quickly discovered, hospitality is not just an idea, but a way of life. Just before the border town of Doğubayazıt, they camped near the Ishak Pasha Palace, which perches precariously on a rock ledge. Built over the 17th and 18th centuries by a Georgian family dynasty, it spoke of former greatness and power. However, it was not the palace that captured the trio's attention so much as a Kurdish shepherd named Ahmed, who lived in a humble dwelling nearby. A spontaneous conversation turned into a heartfelt invitation to dinner, during which the shepherd spoke of the hardships faced by the Kurdish minority in Turkey.

Yet anyone who assumes that Turkish (or Kurdish) hospitality is unparalleled has never been to Iran. The family was overwhelmed by the efforts of ordinary Iranians to welcome their foreign guests, and invitations to tea or dinner were often extended. A particular highlight of their time in Iran was Nowruz, the Persian New Year festival, which occurred while the family was in Tabriz, in northern Iran. The holiday, which usually falls around March 21, marks the beginning of spring and the new year in the Persian calendar, and is traditionally celebrated with various rituals and festive activities, including the ceremonial cleaning and decorating of homes, the preparation of traditional dishes, the lighting of fires, visits from friends and relatives, and the exchange of gifts. Often, these festivities include picnics in the park under the first warming rays of the sun. Chicken skewers with lavash—an Iranian flatbread perfect for wrapping food—are typically served, along with a rich dessert buffet filled with aromatic and traditional delicacies.

After days of celebration, the road beckoned once more. From Tabriz there was a brief stopover in the capital, Tehran, before the journey took Akela on through the semiarid Iranian Plateau, marked by plains and gentle hills interspersed with dry riverbeds. The cities of Isfahan and Yazd shimmered in the landscape; like improbable oases, these places have flourished thanks to agricultural production and artificial irrigation systems. The architecturally stunning historic buildings and well-preserved old towns made strolling a pleasure, even in rising temperatures. The final stop on the mainland was the port city of Bandar Abbas in southern Iran, from where it is possible to take a ferry to nearby Qeshm Island, home to a UNESCO Global Geopark, among other attractions.

The further south they traveled, the drier and hotter the climate, and the more desert-like the landscape became. At one point, Akela got stuck in the sand of Dasht-e Lut, one of the largest salt deserts in the world—it took hours for the family to dig the truck out. They were fortunate it wasn't summer, as Dasht-e Lut's temperatures can reach upwards of 159 degrees Fahrenheit (70 degrees Celsius), making it one of the hottest places in the world. It's a surreal and otherworldly landscape characterized by vast salt flats, sand dunes, barren mountains, and geological formations known as *kaluts.* The colors in this wild, lunar place vary depending on the time of day and range from the bright-white tones of the salt flats to the warm hues of the dunes and the darker shades of the surrounding mountains.

Though finally back on the road, the family was denied entry visas to Turkmenistan, which meant a detour of almost 2,000 miles (3,219 kilometers) to stay on course. But while the flow of life in this part of the world can be unpredictable, for good or ill, it reaffirmed the fact that with some help, ingenuity, and serious determination, there is usually a work-around.

BALKANS

# Striking out: Austria to Croatia, then along the Balkan Range to Greece

Traveling east through the former Yugoslavia to arrive at the ancient seat of the Muses

They took long walks on the deserted beaches, and let themselves be soothed to sleep at night by the sounds of the sea.

———————

The Gulf of Corinth separates the Greek mainland from the Peloponnese. This 81-mile (130-kilometer) coast features idyllic retreats and rocky coves. A path leads through lush vegetation to the sea, where a natural arch stands like a grand gate (opposite). Maria floats in the clear, turquoise-hued Ionian Sea, enjoying the warm summer as gentle waves cradle her (above).

# The Floating Monasteries of Meteora

---

Meteora lies in the heart of Greece, near the town of Kalabaka in the region of Thessaly. It is world-renowned for its Eastern Orthodox monasteries, built between the 14th and 16th centuries on top of majestic rock formations. The rising morning mist gives these sacred sites a mystical aura, leaving the viewer in a state of reverential awe. Today, six of these monasteries remain active and inhabited (opposite). The ascending morning sun casts a halo-like glow over the rocks, enhancing the sublime atmosphere of this unique location (above).

24

Winter painted the land
in a stark but fascinating light.

On a frosty winter day along the Croatian coast, the truck is struggling to start, and Leander tries to get to the bottom of the problem (above left). The crackling fire in the woodstove protects the family from the biting temperatures prevailing outside on this starry night (opposite).

MIDDLE EAST

## Vistas of Mountains, Mosques, and Minarets

From fairy chimneys in Anatolia to semiarid plains
shimmering with oases

MIDDLE EAST

A stunning view of Istanbul unfolds: the Galata Bridge, which spans the Golden Horn, with the Sultan Ahmed (or Blue) Mosque behind it (opposite). The truck's deep tracks mark the Dasht-e Lut Desert, with an abandoned fortress in the background (above).

The further south they traveled, the drier and hotter
the climate, and the more desert-like the landscape became.

———————

# One Thousand and One Nights

---

The Valley of Stars, situated on Qeshm Island—the largest in the Persian Gulf—is a fascinating geological site famous for its extraordinary sandstone formations. Over millennia, erosion and weathering have sculpted these bizarre and surreal rock formations, which resemble structures from another world. Particularly at sunrise or sunset, the Valley of Stars unveils a breathtaking backdrop (opposite). The area is renowned for its hot and dry desert climate, making it an ideal habitat for adaptable camels (above).

In Turkey, the Akela crew quickly discovered, hospitality is not just an idea, but a way of life.

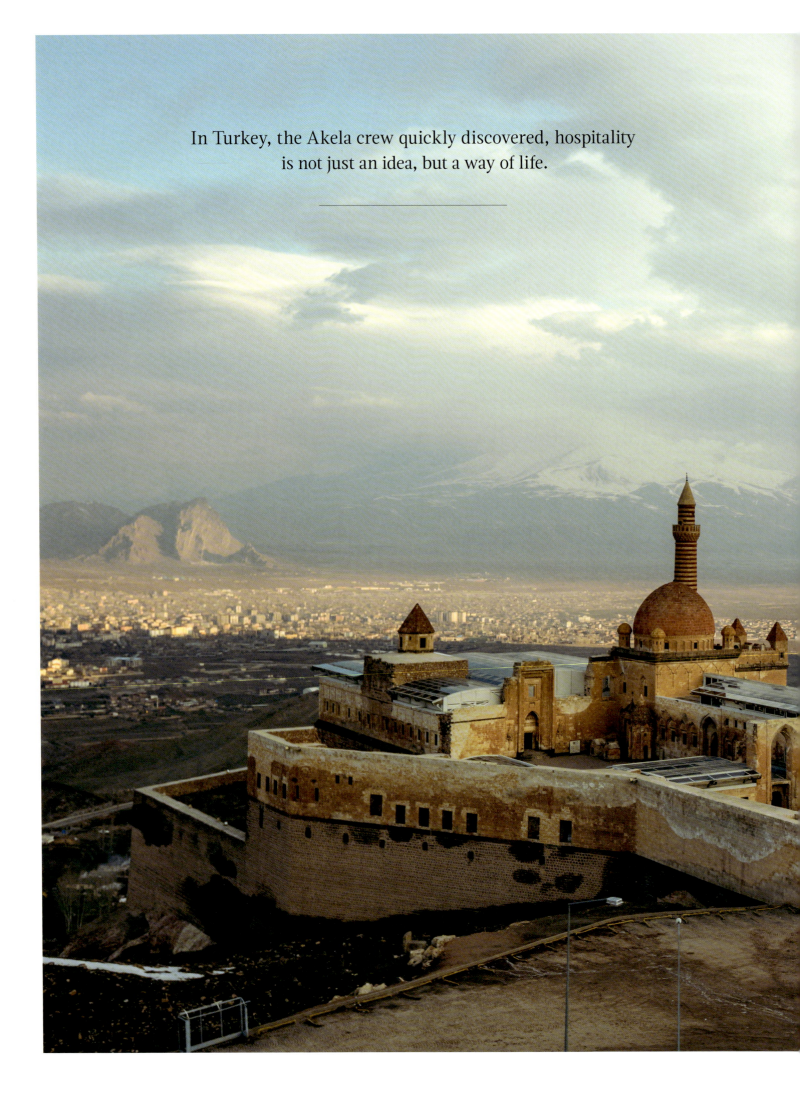

MIDDLE EAST

Dasht-e Lut is a surreal and otherworldly landscape characterized by geological formations known as *kaluts.*

---

A richly decorated temple entrance in Isfahan (above left). Iranian bazaars burst with flavor, and Farsi labels hint at delicious treats (above right). Akela travels a road bordering the Lut Desert, thought to be one of the world's hottest places (opposite).

# Nomadic Life and Nature's Infinite Variety in the Vastness of Central Asia, Russia, and Mongolia

A journey through mountain passes, across open steppes, and along the shores of deep, cold lakes

From mid-May to late November, the journey continued east through the breathtaking landscapes of Kazakhstan, Uzbekistan, Tajikistan, and Kyrgyzstan.

With the help of a car ferry across the Caspian Sea, Akela landed at Kazakhstan, the largest landlocked country in the world. Although the landscape of Kazakhstan is quite varied, the route the trio drove offered little in the way of surprise: endless steppe and plains stretching as far as the eye could see, with dry, brown soil supporting a few thin grasses and bushes inhabited by ground squirrels.

Various ethnic groups live in the dry steppe land, notably Kazakhs, whose rich nomadic culture dates back thousands of years. Kazakhs are a proud people, and horses are an essential part of their modest lives—whether as transportation, work animals, trading goods, or sources of meat. It is unsurprising if a Kazakh learns to ride before they can walk. The close family bonds in small villages and their deep connection to their animals and nature are fundamental to enduring the harsh living conditions.

The trio made a stop at the Aral Sea, hoping for a refreshing dip, but what they found was distressing. Once one of the world's largest lakes, the Aral Sea has shrunk by 50 percent in the last half century, a man-made disaster resulting from unsustainable cotton farming. Abandoned, rusted ships bear witness to what was once a flourishing oasis.

The landscape the family initially encountered in Uzbekistan appeared more barren than in Kazakhstan. A vast, endless expanse stretched before them—no grasses, no shrubs, just desert as far as the eye could see. Various shades of tan and brown alternated and mingled with the blue sky on the horizon. A section of the ancient Silk Road, the former trade route between China and the Mediterranean, once passed through this region—perhaps Marco Polo found better road conditions with his camel caravans than the family did. One pothole followed another, and some were so deep that Akela could have fallen into them. Maria had back pain for two weeks from all the shaking in the cab.

However, upon reaching the cities of Samarkand, Khiva, and Bukhara, the scenery changed dramatically. The widespread brown of the desert faded and was replaced by eye-catching items in a rainbow of hues, from colorful cloths and banners to flowers, gorgeous garments, and splendidly decorated stalls. Life was bustling in the bazaars. The architecture in Uzbekistan is adaptive to the climate—structures are built for comfort in extreme temperatures and dry conditions. Thick walls, shady courtyards, and domes keep homes temperate, while water basins and gardens contribute to cooling.

While the roads in Tajikistan did not improve, the topography changed dramatically. Powerful mountain ranges loomed in the distance shortly after crossing the border. About 93 percent of the country consists of mountains; these include the snow-capped Pamir and Tian Shan ranges, whose tallest peaks reach over 22,966 feet (7,000 meters). In between are fertile valleys with raging rivers, where rustic villages sit along the riverbanks.

As Akela rolled through the landscape, the family marveled at the scenes around them: women laughing as they washed clothes by the river, field workers joyfully waving at them, and excited children running alongside the truck. Despite harsh living conditions, people seemed happy. They owned little, worked hard, and provided for their families with the strength of their hands. They led a self-determined life, far removed from the comforts many cherish.

Faced with this simpler and more honest way of life also opened the family to new experiences. They felt an inner deceleration and gradually adapted to the pace of life around them. The common ailments of the modern world—burnout, deadlines, technology overload, status anxiety, and isolation—held no significance here. Values like family, community, and solidarity were what mattered, and Leander, Maria, and Lennox liked this attitude. The hospitality they encountered in Central Asia was unique. Wherever they stopped, they were warmly welcomed.

One particular highlight in Tajikistan was the start of the Pamir Highway, the second-highest international highway in the world. At 15,272 feet (4,655 meters), the road's Ak-Baital Pass is among the highest drivable passes globally. Due to the poor (and steadily worsening) road conditions, the 10-ton (9,072-kilogram) truck barely managed to exceed 9 mph (14.5 km/h), and that over several days. But Akela's efforts paid off: vast plateaus, nestled among the surrounding peaks, eventually unfolded. The sky was azure blue and within arm's reach, and for the first time, they felt truly free and independent. Simultaneously, the snow-capped peaks of the Pamir Mountains filled them with deep reverence, making them realize just how small and insignificant they were.

Kyrgyzstan was the family's last destination among the "-stan countries," and its beauty revealed itself within just miles of crossing the border. In the distance, the peaks of the Tian Shan Mountains shimmered, with the highest, Pobeda, standing at 24,406 feet (7,439 meters). In addition to numerous glaciers, Kyrgyzstan is blessed with many stunning alpine lakes (many of them glacier-fed), including Ysyk-Köl, one of the largest mountain lakes in the world by volume and renowned for crystal clear waters and inviting shores. The tranquility and isolation of this fantastic place gave the family the time to process their newly acquired impressions, which is so important when traveling for long periods.

Between the mountain ranges lie green valleys and meadows, crisscrossed by rivers and streams. These rich lands are often used for raising animals and growing crops.

The family spent several days at Song-Köl, a lake located on a high plateau 9,895 feet (3,016 meters) above sea level. There, the family traded their vehicle for horses for several days, exploring the lush green meadows and valleys adorned with edelweiss flowers on extensive rides.

Although summer might seem idyllic in this high region, the cold brings many challenges—especially during the harsh winter months, when hungry wolves threaten livestock.

Eagle hunters still train eagles to protect their livestock from wolves—if necessary, an eagle can kill a wolf to ensure the survival of vital herds. Unfortunately, traditions like these are gradually disappearing in today's world. The youth are drawn to the big cities, meaning fewer and fewer people have the knowledge and the skills to carry on the practice. It saddened the family deeply to listen to the words of an eagle hunter telling them about his vanishing tradition.

Autumn approached, bringing cooler temperatures. To avoid traveling through the worst of the winter in Siberia and Mongolia, where temperatures of -58 degrees Fahrenheit (-50 degrees Celsius) are commonplace, the family had to plan ahead and move on. The cold in these regions poses significant challenges for the local population, requiring special clothing, heating methods, and other adjustments, such as not turning off a car's engine overnight. Certainly, vodka helps too.

Not yet in the depths of winter, the family drove through the Altai Mountains, a captivating range spanning parts of Russia, Mongolia, China, and Kazakhstan, where thick forests of tall pines seemed to unfold forever. People once told stories about spirits living in the woods, gods on the mountains, and other mysterious creatures. In the traditional belief systems of the region's Indigenous peoples, the mountains and forests are the dwellings of gods and guardian spirits. Shamans communicate with these otherworldly beings to seek healing, protection, and spiritual guidance for their people. In folkloric tradition, the Altai Mountains are also believed to be the home of a yeti-like creature called an *almas*.

For the family, one of the most striking differences between the -stan countries they drove through and Russia was the roads. Quickly, the desolate tracks transformed into asphalt highways in Russia, which ensured a less stressful driving experience. These roads meandered along vast riverbeds and seemingly endless forested areas, and the family often went days without encountering other souls. The few houses they passed were small, made of wood, and practical in character with only little adornment.

The border between Russia and Western Mongolia was frictionless, and soon the foothills of the Altai Mountains created a breathtaking backdrop of tall grassy hills, deep gorges, and vast steppes traversed by nomadic herds, wild camels, and Przewalski's horses. Some distance from the border lay several significant lakes, including Khar Lake, one of two "black lakes" in the region, which is situated in remote and sparsely populated Western Mongolia, surrounded by dramatic desert and towering sand dunes. The surroundings appeared wild and untouched and were difficult to get to in the truck. Rough terrain and deep sand tracks made the journey a challenge, yet the effort was worth it. Rarely had the family found themselves in such a surreal landscape: a radiant blue sky; golden-brown, almost glowing sand; the glistening lake in the sun; and in the midst of it all, speechless, were Leander, Maria, and Lennox.

The rural roads in Western Mongolia presented new challenges for Akela: their rough, well-worn dirt tracks wound across the plains, occasionally requiring the family to cross unstable and dangerous bridges—occasionally the ground was so uneven in its elevation that the truck was forced to travel at frightening angles. But the effort led to an encounter along the way with a Mongolian nomad, who gestured for the family to follow him to his yurt. He rode ahead, and the three followed him in the truck. Eventually, the nomad stopped in front of a yurt surrounded by yaks. He lived there with his wife,

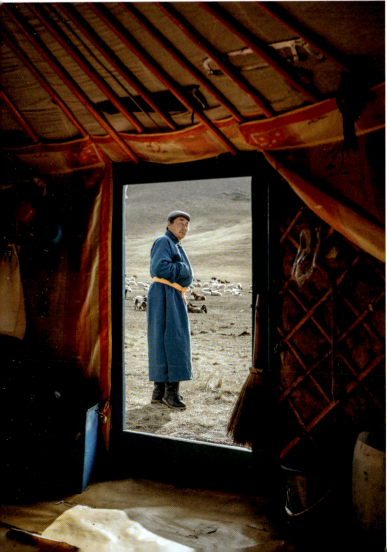

daughter, and grandchild. No words were needed, but the trio felt warmly welcomed and were invited to eat with them. Inside the simply furnished yurt, one of the women cooked a soup in a large pot over an open fire, and warm yak milk was served. The family were honored to be guests of this family and savored every moment—however, they graciously declined the offer of breakfast (dried chicken feet and hard bread) the following morning. After exchanging yak meat for honey, their journey continued.

Passing through the towns of Uliastai and Bayanbulak, the family eventually reached Ulaanbaatar, the capital of Mongolia. Compared to the landscapes they had just driven through, the large and lively city, with its combination of ancient and modern architecture, shops, fast-food restaurants, schools, and universities struck them as extraordinary. Happily, they also found a garage where they could fix their subframe, which had broken along the journey owing to bad road conditions. Sergei, a Russian engineer living with his wife outside the city, was able to help. The family parked Akela on his private property, where Sergei, along with a friend, created the "Russian construction" which holds the subframe together today. The trio greatly appreciated this approach to life—solving problems efficiently with limited resources.

Crossing the border with Russia again led them through the city of Ulan-Ude to Lake Baikal, the deepest and perhaps oldest lake in the world. After a few days of rest on its shores, the family embarked on a 1,800-mile (3,000-kilometer) journey through Siberia, aiming for the Russian port city of Vladivostok.

A significant part of Siberia is covered by the taiga, one of the world's largest contiguous forested areas, predominantly consisting of spruce, pine, larch, and birch. The Siberian tiger also stalks the region. Only in the east did larger cities like Khabarovsk appear on the route, culminating in the fascinating metropolis of Vladivostok, a city known for its maritime atmosphere, rich history, and dynamic development. With its unique location, it serves as a symbolic bridge between Russia and the Asia-Pacific region, the family's next stop.

The family later agreed that their journey across Central Asia, Russia, and Mongolia was the most important and impactful of the entire worldwide trip. The contentment of the people they encountered deeply inspired them, and they gained a new perspective on life. This experience also taught them to appreciate the value of simplicity and find new ways to move forward with the insights they had gained along the way.

CENTRAL ASIA

# Roaming through Kazakhstan, Uzbekistan, Tajikistan, and Kyrgyzstan

Traversing ancient trade routes and high-altitude passes, headed toward lush meadows

A drive along the Pamir Highway (here at over 9,800 feet/3,000 meters) offers a breathtaking view of the snow-capped peaks of the Pamir Mountains (opposite). The sunset over the Charyn Canyon in Kazakhstan presents a majestic backdrop of red sandstone cliffs. This site (above) is often compared to the Grand Canyon in the United States.

Two farmers plow their field with a team of oxen along the 217-mile (350-kilometer) Wakhan Corridor connecting Afghanistan, Tajikistan, Pakistan, and ultimately China (opposite). From Tajikistan, a stunning vista follows the Panj River into Afghanistan, with the snow-capped peaks of the Hindu Kush in the background (above).

The family felt an inner deceleration and gradually adapted to the pace of life around them.

Traditional yurts (above) line the shores of the picturesque Song-Köl Lake in Kyrgyzstan, a gem at an altitude of 9,843 feet (3,000 meters). A proud eagle hunter from Kyrgyzstan presents his traditional attire in a striking portrait. On his hand sits Karajan, a 15-pound (7-kilogram) eagle that helps protect his herds during winter (opposite).

About 93 percent of Tajikistan consists of mountains; these include the snow-capped Pamir and Tian Shan ranges.

CENTRAL ASIA

## *Bright Colors along the Ancient Silk Road*

A view through a richly decorated entrance gate into a mosque in Bukhara, one of Uzbekistan's oldest and most historic cities. Along the ancient Silk Road, trade once flourished, reflected in buildings with elaborate stucco work and intricate ornaments. Preferred colors were blue, especially turquoise and gold, showcasing the builders' wealth. Bukhara's mosques are Islamic architectural masterpieces, impressive for their size, structure, and detailed decoration (opposite). Akela, perfectly matching the domes and intricate design work, stands in front of a mosque's entrance gate in the middle of Bukhara (above).

The snow-capped peaks of the Pamir Mountains filled them with deep reverence, making them realize just how small and insignificant they were.

RUSSIA & MONGOLIA

# Weaving between Russia and Mongolia on the road to Vladivostok

Tall pine forests, towering sand dunes, and
wild horses in the long shadow of Genghis Khan

The deep blue of Tolbo Lake and the golden sand shimmering in the sun lend the scenery a unique dreamlike ambiance (opposite). Located in western Mongolia in the Bayan-Ölgii Province, the lake sits at an altitude of 6,820 feet (2,080 meters) and impresses with its clear water (above).

RUSSIA & MONGOLIA

# *The Desert Is Alive*

A sudden rainbow casts a surreal appearance over Khar Nuur, a lake in western Mongolia's Zavkhan Province. This region's vast, weathered landscapes make travel difficult and require driving on some of Mongolia's toughest roads. Along the southern shore, the lake's color changes with the light—amethyst, jade, emerald, silver, and turquoise. Nestled between the Bor Khyarin sand dunes, the freshwater lake (opposite) is an important bird sanctuary. During hikes through the golden-brown dunes, Lennox discovers scorpions, snakes, and lizards. The remote tranquility of this unique place captivates the family (above).

The Altai Mountains created a wondrous backdrop to vast steppes. The surroundings appeared wild and untouched.

# Eastbound Escapades in South Korea and Japan

Encountering skyscrapers, feudal architecture,
and magic mountains dusted with snow

---

From Vladivostok, at the eastern edge of Russia, the trio took a ferry to the South Korean port city of Donghae. The three-hour crossing was smooth, but negotiating customs proved to be a challenge—the trio quickly realized that English was of little help. However, with the aid of a translation app and simple gestures, they were able to navigate the various requirements.

In the days that followed, their travels took them through South Korea's densely populated hill towns and valleys into the heart of the country, to the vibrant capital Seoul, a city where modernity and tradition are held in fascinating tension. And later, after a ferry ride from Busan in the southeast to the Japanese port city of Fukuoka, they began their exploration of Kyushu and Honshu.

Early on, the vast geographical, cultural, and economic differences between these countries and those they had recently left was immediately apparent. While Central Asia was dominated by largely remote regions characterized by semi-deserts, steppes, and mountains, here they traversed densely populated countries where space was at a premium. And across both South Korea and Japan, they encountered the kind of state-of-the-art infrastructure and technological innovation both countries are renowned for, alongside rich cultural histories shaped by various faiths.

Nestled in Gangwon Province, Donghae is a tranquil town with around 100,000 inhabitants, situated on the country's eastern coast and bordering the Sea of Japan. So as to get a proper first impression of their new destination, the trio parked the truck outside the city and set off on foot. The hustle and bustle of the city took some time to get used to after the emptiness of the steppe. They were immediately taken aback by the traffic, and the absence of any English-language signage was daunting. The architecture they encountered, however, was diverse and inspiring, reflecting both modern and traditional building styles. Amidst gleaming skyscrapers and shopping centers they found traditional wooden houses with curved roofs and ornate decoration.

The family then traveled northwest to Seoraksan National Park, located within the Taebaek Mountains, a range that extends across both North and South Korea. Seoraksan Park includes the impressive Daecheongbong Peak, which towers above the landscape at 5,604 feet (1,708 meters). The family stayed and hiked in the park for several days, basking in the dramatic views. From there, they headed to the neon-lit capital of Seoul.

With approximately 10 million inhabitants, Seoul is the cultural, economic, and political center of the country, with an urban topography punctuated by traditional sights (like Gyeongbokgung Palace, which dates back to 1395), and ultra-modern architecture, typified by the group of skyscrapers in the Gangnam District. The family visited traditional markets, which are often housed in vast, covered halls, and where, alongside traditional kimchi—a spicy mix of fermented vegetables seasoned with garlic, ginger, chili, and salt—there were huge amounts of fish to marvel at, alongside dried stingrays and other varieties of seafood. They stayed in Seoul for a week before venturing southeast to the other end of the island. From Busan, they took a ferry to their next destination: Japan.

Their Japanese odyssey began on Kyushu, one of the country's four main islands—they started out in the city of Fukuoka. Navigating Japanese cities was easier, especially in major urban areas, where street signs and traffic signals were often available in English. Just as in South Korea, the Japanese cities impressively balanced ancient and modern traditions. First on the itinerary was Aso-Kujū National Park, home to the mighty active volcano, Mount Aso, which boasts one of the world's largest calderas. Here were breathtaking landscapes, offering picturesque views of green valleys and the massive double crater.

The region is also renowned for its hot springs, known as *onsen,* whose mineral-rich waters provide visitors with relaxation and rejuvenation. Both natural and man-made *onsen* share a surprising common bathing custom: the strict separation between men and women. The family's final stop on Kyushu was the historic city of Iwakuni, famous for its Kintai Bridge. Constructed in the late 17th century, it consists of five wooden arches that, for the bridge's first 300 years, held together without the use of metal nails.

The family continued their journey to the northern island of Honshu, passing through densely populated urban areas like Hiroshima, forever marked by the tragedy of the atomic bomb, and Okayama. As they traveled overland, their eyes roved over mountains, valleys, and agricultural fields still in the grip of winter.

The breathtaking and carefully preserved Himeji Castle greeted them from its hilltop perch in Himeji, Hyōgo Prefecture, its structure a showcase for typical Japanese fortification architecture. Built in the 16th century, this fortress has been a UNESCO World Heritage Site since 1993, offering an unparalleled glimpse into feudal Japanese culture.

The journey took them next to Kobe, a large port city whose architectural history dates back to the Meiji era. From there they traveled to Osaka, Japan's buzzing economic and cultural hub, and finally to Kyoto, famous for its temples and Shinto shrines, where they were forced to stay several weeks in a garage in order to fix a broken heater. Their Japanese mechanics, Ko and Kyoshi, worked tirelessly with Leander on the heating system, resulting in a friendship.

Eventually, and with a newly repaired heater, the trio proceeded north, encountering increasing amounts of snow as they drove. Mountain peaks were blanketed in fluffy white powder, transforming the landscape into a sparkling fairy-tale world. As passionate skiers, a stopover in Hakuba, one of Japan's largest ski resorts (and one of the sites of the 1998 Winter Olympics), was a must. Snow fell continuously for several days, resulting in immense drifts that required clearing Akela's roof multiple times a day to prevent it from collapsing under the heavy load. Even so, getting to ski Japan's famously soft powder was more than worth these small inconveniences.

As their time in Japan slowly reached an end, they began to retrace their steps along the same route they had taken. After a brief stay in Kyoto, where they greeted friends, the family headed south to the small town of Kōyasan. On Mount Kōya, amidst towering cedar trees, lies one of Japan's oldest and largest cemeteries—Okunoin. It serves not only as a resting place for Japanese warlords, noble families, philosophers, and poets, but as a Buddhist pilgrimage site. The trio visited at various times of day, with each time eliciting profoundly different emotions.

With a final visit to the Engyō-ji monastery, which featured in the 2003 film *The Last Samurai,* the trio concluded their time in Japan. Once back in Osaka, they made their final preparations to ship Akela to Borneo.

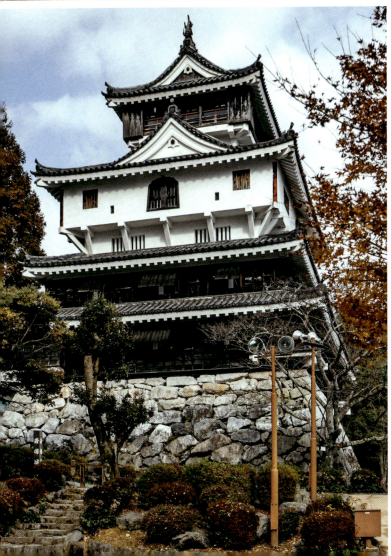

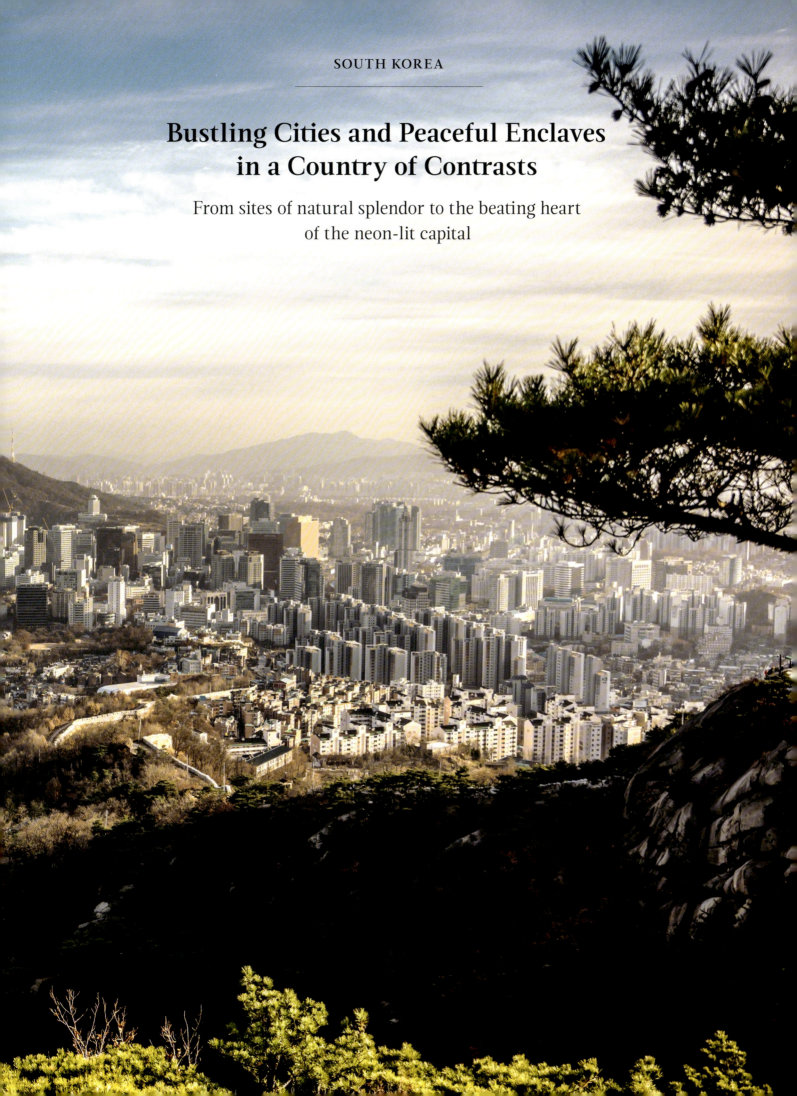

SOUTH KOREA

# Bustling Cities and Peaceful Enclaves in a Country of Contrasts

From sites of natural splendor to the beating heart of the neon-lit capital

The trio encountered state-of-the-art infrastructure, alongside rich cultural histories shaped by various faiths.

SOUTH KOREA

## *An Elegant Blend of Modernity and Tradition*

---

A stroll through suburban Seoul in mild spring weather reveals a serene contrast to the nearby bustling city center. Here, one can find typical traditional houses, known as *hanok,* which utilize natural materials such as wood, paper, and clay, and feature curved roofs and intricate decorations (above). Although Koreans are sometimes socially reserved, it didn't stop this trio from smiling warmly in their colorful garments (opposite).

JAPAN

# Into Magical Wintry Wonderlands

Volcanoes, hot springs,
and skiing in snowy, enchanted lands

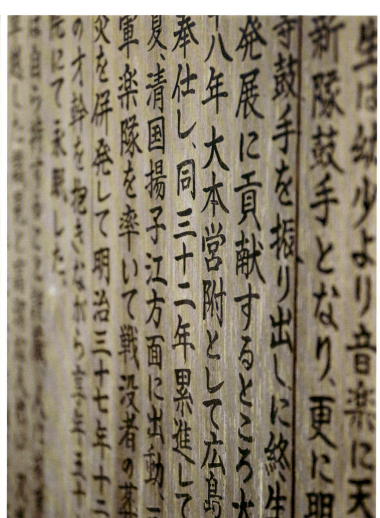

The Fushimi Inari Shrine in the city of Kyoto was founded in the year 711 BCE and is among the 30,000-plus Inari shrines found throughout Japan (opposite). The shrine is famous for its thousands of brightly colored red torii gates (above).

Mountain peaks were blanketed in fluffy
white powder, transforming the landscape into
a sparkling fairy-tale world.

A breathtaking view of the snow-covered mountains of Hakuba in Nagano Prefecture,
an outdoor paradise for winter-sports enthusiasts and one of the sites of the 1998 Winter
Olympics (opposite). An impressive shrine and gateway deity near Kōyasan (above).

## A Forest Bath Among Rustling Bamboo Stalks

A path through a bamboo forest outside the bustling city of Kyoto. The tall, densely packed bamboo stalks create a peaceful, almost otherworldly atmosphere, especially when the wind gently rustles them. Bamboo is known for its resilience and flexibility—it bends in the wind without breaking, symbolizing strength and adaptability. A walk through this bamboo forest evokes a deep sense of connection with nature. The simplicity and beauty of the landscape invite visitors to focus on what truly matters and to appreciate the natural world in all its splendor.

# A Multi-Stage Sojourn among the Dense Rainforests of Borneo and Indonesia

Traversing Borneo's Wild Heart to Java's Fiery Volcanic Realms

While the family traveled by plane, a cargo ship transported Akela from Osaka to Kota Kinabalu, a Malaysian city on the island of Borneo. Covered in tropical rainforest and the third-largest island in the world, Borneo is home to three sovereign countries: Malaysia, Brunei, and Indonesia. In the bustling Malaysian city of Kota Kinabalu, or KK for short, the trio picked up their truck and spent a few days at a public beach, acclimating to the tropical summer. From KK they drove northeast through the Malaysian state of Sabah to the Tip of Borneo, the northernmost point of the island, where they enjoyed untouched beaches and grand views of both the South China and Sulu seas. The sense that they had reached paradise was dampened, however, by the visible military presence and an awareness of the area's history of political violence.

Passing southeast through small villages and well-paved, palm-lined roads, they eventually reached the town of Sandakan, an ideal base for expeditions to the Sepilok Orangutan Rehabilitation Centre, as well as other conservation areas along the Kinabatangan River. Borneo's rainforests, maintained by each of the three countries, harbor many unique creatures. Along the banks of the Kinabatangan alone, the family spotted proboscis monkeys, wild orangutans, and a variety of bird species, including hornbills, kingfishers, and ospreys. But the state of Borneo's wildlife is precarious: due to the uncontrolled deforestation that occurs when clearing land for palm oil plantations, vast areas of these creatures' natural habitat have disappeared. Many native species have lost their homes and been threatened with extinction—this includes Borneo's shaggy mascot, the orangutan. During their visit, the family felt fortunate to see a few of these great apes in the wild.

Upon reaching Semporna, a town close to some of the world's best diving islands, the family had an eye-opening encounter with the nomadic Bajau Laut—a sea-dwelling people living off the coast in stilt houses or in traditional boats called *lepa*. Without citizenship and basic rights, these people lead a minimalist existence in harmony with nature, relying on fishing and occasional trade for their livelihood. In recent years, tourism has become an additional, if not entirely welcome, source of income.

After returning to KK, the family's journey took them through Brunei to the Malaysian state of Sarawak and the city of Kuching, which boasts another center (Semenggoh) dedicated to orangutan rehabilitation. Crossing the border into Indonesia, they then drove through the Kalimantan region, crossed the earth's equator at Pontianak, and finally reached the city of Surabaya, on the main island of Java, by ferry. This marked the beginning of their one-year stay in Indonesia, which took them island hopping from Java to Bali, Lombok, and eventually Sumbawa.

While they had found the natural landscapes of South Korea and Japan to be mainly characterized by wooded hills, steep mountain ranges, and rugged coves, Borneo and Indonesia appeared as true green oases, rich with dense rainforests, wide rivers, and long coastal plains enlivened by a variety of caves, waterfalls, and mangrove forests. These topographic differences were often accompanied, however, by challenging road conditions and heavy traffic. While city roads were kind to Akela, in rural areas the family often encountered gravel or dirt tracks with bottlenecks, potholes, herds of livestock, and low-hanging power lines—all of which made maneuvering difficult. Also, extreme rainfall and flash floods could transform a road within minutes.

Islam is the dominant religion in Borneo and Indonesia, and during Ramadan, from dawn until sunset, people refrain from eating, drinking, smoking, and other worldly pleasures, while prayers echo from the speakers of mosques. On most days, the family witnessed life unfolding outdoors and in the streets in vibrant, vivid cacophony, underpinned by ideals of kindness and communal support. In the local cooking they found a similar ethos, as curry, turmeric, cumin, and coriander combined to create an explosion of flavor.

Having only traveled through countries with four seasons, the family now had to adapt to the idea of eternal summer and the constant tropical heat. Naturally, these climate conditions affect the flora and fauna, and in Borneo, everything seemed especially fecund and large. Hand-sized butterflies, finger-thick ants, huge spiders, and other creepy-crawlies teemed in the lush vegetation. Rainforest trees, palms, and ferns shone in a variety of green shades, while the cries and calls of animals entered Akela's open windows. The family often caught sight of monkeys, snakes, and lizards, even on the roads. Despite all of the beauty and seeming abundance, it was once again impossible to ignore the effects of deforestation and development on the land, which has led to the disappearance of Indigenous peoples and significant losses in animal biodiversity.

Island hopping on old car ferries was a budget-friendly way to travel between the many islands, even Borneo to Java. Java, the main island of the 17,000-island Indonesian archipelago, sits on a roiling ring of fire. The two most famous active volcanoes, Mount Bromo and Mount Ijen, are both located here. Ijen, the sulfur mountain, is known not only for its impressive blue crater lake, which shines like a sapphire amid the smoking caldera, but also for brutal labor conditions: every night, workers descend deep into the crater, mining sulfur by hand and carrying large loads of it out on their shoulders.

The journey continued to the majority-Hindu island of Bali, the "pearl" of the Indian Ocean, also known as a holiday destination for Australians and a pilgrimage site for hippies, yogis, and artists seeking self-discovery. Beneath the tourist trappings, the island's true face is also visible, in the form of countless waterfalls, beautifully terraced rice fields, and majestic temple complexes. The family was disturbed to find Bali, along with its neighboring islands Lombok and Sumbawa, struggling under huge amounts of plastic waste mostly generated by the increasing influx of tourists. Both land and sea bore the brunt, yet with patience and a discerning eye, pristine beaches could still be found. At these hidden gems, the world seemed bursting with life, both above and below water. During a snorkeling trip off the small island of Nusa Penida, for example, the family encountered a squadron of manta rays with wingspans of up to 26 feet (8 meters), swimming within arm's reach.

On Lombok, aside from a few tourist hotspots, the island was relatively quiet and serene. The exception was during Ramadan, when the prayers of the muezzins called from every mosque loudspeaker until late into the night. Restful sleep was out of the question, at least until sunrise. The family also discovered that many shops and service providers kept their doors closed during the fasting month, in order to devote themselves more fully to the religious ritual.

On the island of Sumbawa, the adventurers immersed themselves one last time in the archipelago's gorgeous coral reefs. For now six-year-old Lennox, it was an especially moving snorkeling experience. Afterwards, he expressed his fear that if people continued to ignore the plight of the oceans, his own children would not get to experience their beauty, a sentiment which made his parents both proud and sad: proud that their young son showed such awareness and concern, and sad that someone so young should have to worry about these things.

Back on the main island of Java, they had to follow a rigorous, six-week cleaning process to prepare Akela for Australia's quarantine and entry regulations. Before delivering Akela at the port, they did some sightseeing around the city of Yogyakarta, including Borobudur Temple, the largest Buddhist temple in the world. Borobudur stands impressively on a hill surrounded by mountains and volcanoes, and its awe-inspiring stone architecture features nine stacked platforms, many stupas, and thousands of relief panels.

Finally, it was time to bid farewell to the truck, this time for five weeks. Once again, Akela set sail alone, this time bound for Melbourne, Australia.

BORNEO

# Acclimating to Eternal Summer

Relaxed lifestyles and world-class
diving on the third-largest island in the world

Sepilok Nature Lodge near the Orangutan Rescue Centre in the Indonesian part of Borneo (opposite).
A rescued orangutan at the rehabilitation facility in the district of Sabah (above). Although native to Indonesia
and Malaysia, these unique creatures are now only found on Borneo and Sumatra.

## The Sea Dwellers

---

The Bajau Laut, also known as sea nomads, inhabit the waters surrounding Indonesia, Malaysia, and the Philippines. They spend most of their lives there, residing in simple traditional stilt houses or boats. An ethnic minority, they live without rights, passports, or citizenship. Yet thanks to their extraordinary underwater skills, they are adept hunters, providing sustenance for their families. Often, multiple generations coexist within a single stilt house or on a boat, fostering a sense of security and unity.

Rainforest trees, palms, and ferns shone in a
variety of green shades, while the cries and calls
of animals entered Akela's open windows.

---

The Niah Caves (opposite) are located deep in the heart of Sarawak, the Malaysian part of Borneo. They are famous for their archaeological significance, particularly for the discovery of human remains, such as the Deep Skull, an "anatomically modern" skull almost 40,000 years old. On the way to the caves, visitors encounter a variety of birds, including this majestic kingfisher (above left).

INDONESIA

## Vibrant Life on Land and in the Sea

Stilt houses, terraced rice fields,
and postcard beaches on Indonesia's islands

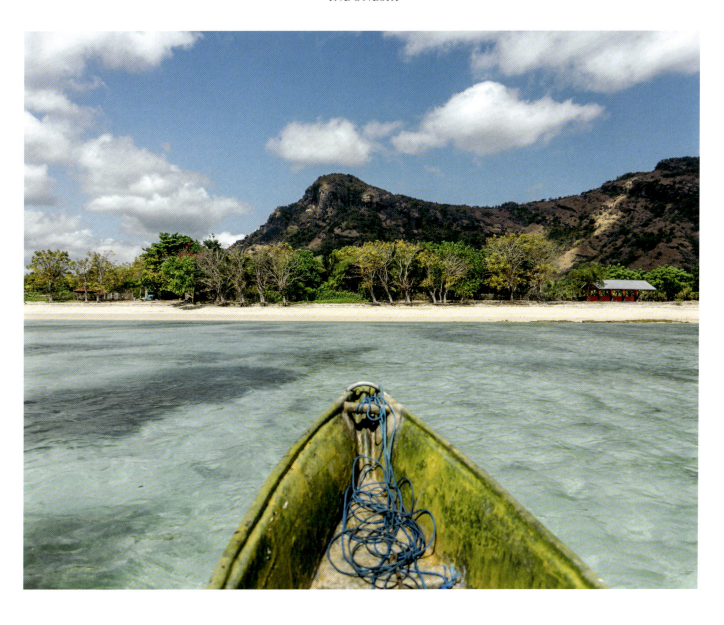

Snorkeling along the unique coastlines of the island of Sumbawa (opposite).
Together with a local fisherman, Leander, Maria, and Lennox
explore the pristine underwater worlds of the Indian Ocean (above).

INDONESIA

# *From a Fiery Ring to a Sublime Temple*

A magnificent early-morning view over the 7,641-foot (2,329-meter) Mount Bromo volcano (opposite). The active volcano is located in Java, Indonesia's main island. The swiftly passing clouds, combined with the obscured sunlight, lend this extraordinary volcanic landscape, situated in the Ring of Fire, a threatening yet mystical touch. Elsewhere, in Central Java, approximately 25 miles (40 kilometers) northwest of Yogyakarta, a similarly mystical, lofty atmosphere is encountered at the vast Borobudur Temple (above), a Buddhist sanctuary constructed from stone blocks without the use of mortar, and consisting of nine terraces forming a pyramid-like structure.

Bali's true face is visible, in the form of countless waterfalls, beautifully terraced rice fields, and majestic temple complexes.

———————————

# A Year Traversing the Many Expanses of Mainland Australia and Tasmania

Unforgettable landscapes, laid-back lifestyles, and wild endemic plants and animals on the red continent

After a year in Central Asia and another in Borneo and Indonesia, Australia came as something of a culture shock to Leander, Maria, and Lennox. The trappings and cultural signposts of the world they had left behind in Europe years before seemed to finally reappear. However, during the year they spent in Australia, they chose to mostly bypass the country's busy metropolises in favor of pristine beaches in Tasmania, enormous, star-filled skies in the outback, bright-pink lakes in Western Australia, and sacred Aboriginal sites in the Northern Territory. Despite these expansive adventures, their time in Australia partially coincided with the country's catastrophic wildfires of 2019–2020, which emphasized anew to them the profound fragility of the natural world.

Before a vehicle can be imported into Australia, it must first undergo a quarantine and thorough cleaning process. These regulations are intended to prevent introduced organisms from disturbing the country's ecological balance and potentially threatening the native species. Happily, Akela successfully passed the inspection at the port of Melbourne, and after a brief respite in the city, they continued their journey to Tasmania via car ferry.

Tasmania is a sparsely populated island of approximately 550,000 people, with plenty of room to set up camp on lonely beaches or amidst blooming lavender fields. The Bay of Fires, located in the northeast of the island, is a particular highlight, notable for its white, sandy beaches, crystal-clear waters, and striking granite and sandstone formations which glow in a variety of red tones at sunrise and sunset. This unique coloration is caused by a high iron content in the rock, but the bay's name in fact derives from the nightly campfires of the Indigenous peoples who once lived there. Surrounding these beaches are lush rainforests with dense vegetation, and the family's hikes through nearby mountains provided stunning views of the surrounding land.

Approximately 12,000 years ago, Tasmania split off from mainland Australia, and in the ensuing years, numerous plants and animals became endemic to the island. One such example is the platypus, a unique, shy, and largely nocturnal mammal that the family was lucky to encounter. It happened like this: one evening, shortly after the sun had set, Leander, Maria, and Lennox, armed with flashlights, ventured along the banks of small streams and rivers, on the prowl for the strange, duck-billed animal. Quietly and with cautious steps, they searched the area. They were about to give up when Lennox let out a quiet cry. He illuminated a spot in the riverbed where a platypus was hiding behind a rock. Unfazed, the creature emerged and revealed its full size.

Back on mainland Australia, their journey took them southward along the legendary Great Ocean Road. This 149-mile (240-kilometer) two-lane road offers breathtaking views of the ocean, rugged cliffs, white-sand beaches, and iconic offshore limestone stacks known as the Twelve Apostles. They stopped at Grampians National Park, which features some peaks of the highest mountains in Australia. While driving through Adelaide in South Australia and up into the heart of the continent—the Red Centre, a section of the outback—they stopped in Coober Pedy, famous worldwide for its opal deposits and unique underground homes. Miners founded the town in the early 19th century, building their homes underground to escape the scorching heat. For many visitors, Coober Pedy is a place of hope, because here, amidst the desert, lies the potential for a lucky discovery in the form of opals. Lennox realized a particular knack for locating these semiprecious stones, rarely having to dig long in the glittering sand before suddenly lifting out a sparkling specimen.

2019 marked the closure of the climbing route at Ayers Rock (or Uluru in the language of the Pitjantjatjara people), 34 years after it was officially handed back to the Aṉangu (a group comprising several Indigenous groups). The sandstone monolith is of course the iconic tourist landmark of Australia, but it is, more importantly, a sacred mountain in the Dreamtime—the spiritual creation period of the Aboriginal people, during which the landscape, animals, and spiritual laws originated. This concept is conveyed through stories, songs, and artworks and is an integral part of Aboriginal peoples' identity and spirituality. The return of Uluru to the Aṉangu in 1985 was a long-awaited and hard-won goal, representing a symbolic act of restitution. The closure of the climbing route was another step in restoring this sacred site. However, these gestures did not change the fact that deep-rooted injustices against Australia's Aboriginal population persist.

Arriving in Western Australia, daily life seemed more relaxed and peaceful. Radio stations played back-to-back rock and pop classics from the '80s, and the locals lived a laid-back lifestyle that the family felt at home with.

Here in the outback, the nickname "red continent" truly came to life: roughly 70 percent of the land is dry and barren and red in hue. The color comes from the iron-rich rock oxidizing at the surface, creating an abundance of red dust that would manage to find its way into every corner of the truck. The corrugated tracks leading through the desert also took some getting used to and required them to endlessly deflate and inflate their tires along the way. Additionally, the outback's sandy roads are shared with the rather intimidating road trains, semitrucks with trailers that can run up to 164 feet (50 meters) long. Caution around these is paramount, as they have considerable mass and can create significant air resistance. There are also traditional trains: often, Akela would wait for what seemed like an eternity at deserted railway crossings before a 1.2-mile-long (2-kilometer-long) freight train passed by, loaded with iron ore and crossing through the heart of the country.

The nighttime ambiance in the outback is characterized by absolute tranquility. The clear starry sky, free from light pollution, reveals shimmering shooting stars traveling through the Milky Way. In this silent landscape, there's an atmosphere of profound grandeur, and it's easy to lose oneself in the infinite expanses of the cosmos.

Splashes of color in the landscape, such as the kind the Pink Lakes provide, offer a welcome sight during the somewhat monotonous drive to the coast of Western Australia. Pink algae are responsible for the water's coloration, and though a feast for the eyes, a swim is inadvisable. These are alkaline lakes and their water can cause severe skin irritation.

After several days of driving, the family finally reached the coast. Their goal was Ningaloo Reef, the second largest in Australia. After traversing a rough corrugated track (and fearing the loss of their motorcycle from the rear rack), they made it to the beach. Depending on the season, you can spot whale sharks, eagle rays, whales, and other extraordinary marine life from Ningaloo. Other surprising encounters might occur on the beach itself: one large pelican, traditionally a very shy bird, approached Lennox and even allowed him to feed it with seaweed.

Kangaroos are often synonymous with Australia, as are their smaller family members, wallabies. The family came to doubt whether the giant red kangaroos actually exist, as they failed to see a single one in their yearlong stay. Instead, they often made their acquaintance with Australia's less-than-delightful saltwater crocodiles, which are found in Western Australia, the Northern Territory, and north Queensland. These rather frightening reptiles inhabit bays, mouths of rivers, mangroves, or the open sea, and they are always on the prowl. Posted signs warned travelers at every turn, and while the ocean was always inviting, Leander, Maria, and Lennox usually kept to extended beach walks.

The Kimberley region, with its rugged wilderness, unusual rock formations, and deep gorges, was also impressive. While there, they became familiar with the Australian boab tree, which shares the same genus as the Madagascar variety but is separated by the Indian Ocean. On a multiday canoe trip, they explored the beauty of the Kimberley region along the Ord River, a paradise for bird lovers. Many of these species are endemic to Australia, including the kookaburra, whose song is often compared to human laughter.

In the Northern Territory, huge termite mounds lined the path to Kakadu National Park, marking the end of the family's west-to-north route. These mounds can reach heights of up to 20 feet (6.1 meter), and in addition to providing a comfortable living environment for lizards, snakes, and birds, they have historically played an important role in the culture of Indigenous people, serving as navigational points and spiritual symbols. Kakadu is also home to the sacred site of Ubirr, which features Aboriginal rock paintings featuring animals, plants, and human figures believed to date back to 30,000 BCE.

For our travelers, the warmth and helpfulness of the Australian people was evident on multiple occasions. Whether it was a problem that needed solving or the dispensing of useful tips, help was always at hand. There was no solution to the intense heat, which in the summer feels unrelenting, sometimes reaching highs above 100 degrees Fahrenheit (40 degrees Celsius). During these months, especially between November and March, it's advisable to prepare for potential bushfires, which are aided by heat-withered vegetation and spread by strong winds. In some places, waterholes along the route provided the only relief from the heat—with the caveat to always check for crocodiles.

Arriving in Sydney, the family was relieved to learn that the immediate threat from the raging bushfires had subsided, yet a journey in the shadow of a natural catastrophe couldn't help but haunt them. After a year full of adventures in Australia, the trio began preparations to ship Akela to America.

TASMANIA

# Finding Tranquility on a Sparsely Populated Island

Blooming lavender fields, fiery red stones, and lush forest in Australia's southeastern island state

TASMANIA

## Surrounded by Elves and Fairies

---

The sun rarely manages to break through the thick canopy of the Tasmanian rainforest. But when it does, magical moments occur (opposite). The Tasmanian rainforest is remarkable for its lush vegetation, which includes centuries-old trees like the Huon pine (above). These temperate rainforests are unique and home to a variety of endemic plant and animal species. They are crucial for preserving biodiversity and offer breathtaking sights. A mindful walk through this forest feels like a balm for the soul.

Tasmania is a sparsely populated island, and this affords travelers the freedom to set up camp on lonely beaches.

A spellbinding view over the Bay of Fires, located on the northeastern coast of Tasmania and marked by its distinctive fiery red rocks (opposite). A close-up of a Tasmanian fern in the rainforest (above left). The echidna, a small, spiny mammal native to Tasmania and Australia, belongs to the group of egg-laying mammals along with the platypus (above right).

Tasmania split off from mainland Australia, and in the ensuing years, numerous plants and animals became endemic to the island.

AUSTRALIA

# Outback and Beyond: Circling Mainland Australia over an Eventful Year

Star-filled skies, pink lakes, and sacred sites
in the land down under

AUSTRALIA

Karijini National Park in Western Australia, where the landscape is marked by
striking red rocks and geological layers of ancient ironstone and sandstone (opposite).
A unique play of colors along the west coast (above).

AUSTRALIA

Four eagle rays just off the west coast (above). An extraordinary drive over Sea Cliff Bridge along the Pacific Ocean. The bridge is part of the Grand Pacific Drive, a scenic route that leads from Sydney to Wollongong and beyond (opposite).

Depending on the season, you can spot whale sharks, eagle rays, whales, and other extraordinary marine life.

AUSTRALIA

## *Martian Landscapes in the Red Centre*

---

Akela took a lonely road between Coober Pedy and Alice Springs en route to the Red Centre (opposite), enjoying spectacular views of the Larapinta Trail in the Northern Territory, near the town of Alice Springs. The trail stretches 137 miles (221 kilometers) and offers majestic views of red desert landscapes, deep canyons, scenic waterholes, and fascinating rock formations. It never gets boring: the outback provides enormous landscape variety, which allows the scorching heat to fade—somewhat—into the background (above).

Different perspectives on the sacred mountain of the Aborigines. Uluru, also known as Ayers Rock, is one of Australia's most famous natural landmarks. Situated in the arid Red Centre of the Northern Territory, this enormous sandstone formation stands 1,142 feet (348 meters) high and has a circumference of 5.8 miles (9.4 kilometers).

In the outback's silent landscape, there's an atmosphere of profound grandeur.

AUSTRALIA

A "beware of kangaroos" sign, found on many roads throughout
Australia (opposite). Akela on a remote beach in South Australia flooded
with the light of the setting sun (above).

# Endless Stories across Canada, the USA, and Mexico

An epic, emotional journey from the Northern Rockies to the Guatemalan border—with an unplanned stop back home in between

---

Akela's shipment from Melbourne, Australia, to Los Angeles, California, took five weeks—the longest leg the truck had undertaken alone. After a seamless customs clearance, the adventure in the land of unlimited possibilities could begin.

The town of Yucca Valley, the family's first stop, serves as a gateway to Joshua Tree National Park. The park's name derives from its distinctive Joshua trees (also known as yucca trees), whose forking branches and tufts of pointed leaves on their tops make them a striking feature of the Southwest desert landscape.

The journey then led them through the Mojave Desert to the breathtaking Monument Valley, whose huge sandstone buttes have become synonymous with the Wild West and have provided the backdrop for many classic Westerns. They continued through northern Arizona to the truly awe-inspiring Grand Canyon and finally to the state of Utah, where they stayed with a family in Salt Lake City, the state capital, and explored the surrounding canyons.

In the spring-green state of Wyoming, they took advantage of numerous climbing opportunities before traveling on to Montana, nicknamed "Big Sky Country," which it more than lives up to. Here, stunning prairies, majestic mountains, crystal clear lakes, and rushing rivers passed by Akela's windows.

Between Grand Teton and Glacier National Park, a chance encounter with a mother grizzly bear and her four cubs—seen from a distance—sweetened their last days in the United States, but while attempting to cross the border into Canada, they were dealt a frustrating setback—due to the growing Covid-19 crisis, they were denied entry by Canadian authorities. When they turned back and tried to re-enter the United States, they were admitted, but were given a 30-day deadline to leave the country. American border officials cited both the pandemic and an overstayed visa as their reasons.

Feeling stressed, the family embarked on a 1,860-mile (2,993-kilometer) marathon drive to the East Coast, where they had to hastily arrange for Akela to be shipped from Baltimore to Europe—their only option. Once back in Europe, the family, like most of the world, felt directionless, stuck. Disheartened by the abrupt end of their adventure, they traveled to Greece, the home of their hearts, which they had left six years before. During the six ensuing months in Greece, they recuperated at their favorite beaches, devising new plans.

With the gradual easing of restrictions on travel, the call of the Americas remained strong, and eight months after their expulsion from the United States, the trio shipped Akela once again, this time from Belgium to Halifax, Nova Scotia in eastern Canada.

Disaster struck again when Akela arrived heavily damaged in Halifax, marking an abrupt pause to their renewed adventures. The truck's clutch and several other parts were broken, and it took over two months to get it back on the road. Once Akela was roadworthy again, the family sped through the provinces of New Brunswick, Québec, Ontario, Manitoba, and Saskatchewan, heading straight for Alberta. Amid the rugged Rocky Mountains, with their deep valleys, glittering glaciers, and clear lakes, the three began to feel at home once more. They spent their days on challenging mountain hikes, enjoying icy dips in glacier lakes and warming themselves by campfires at secluded campsites.

As fall arrived, they took the ferry from Horseshoe Bay to Vancouver Island, arriving just in time for the annual salmon migration. This is an event that provides a feast not just for the bears (who need to build up fat reserves for hibernation), but for eagles and otters—the area's entire ecosystem relies on the abundant feast provided by the salmon run. As passionate divers, the trio donned thick wet suits, braved the icy Pacific waters, and observed orca pods swimming in the distance.

Back on the mainland, deep winter had already set in. The adventurers couldn't resist enjoying some exhilarating days of world-class skiing in Whistler Blackcomb, north of Vancouver, and then at Stevens Pass just over the border in the state of Washington. A raging, several-day storm disrupted their plans to drive leisurely along the U.S. West Coast before a final ski stop in the Tahoe area, forcing them instead to make a swift sprint southward. Within a few days, they drove from Seattle through Portland, down to Sacramento, and then to Los Angeles, before stopping again in Yucca Valley to prepare the truck for the trip to Mexico.

Once south of the border, they cruised along the dreamy, deserted beaches of Baja California, both on the calm, gulf-facing side and on the peninsula's more rugged, Pacific-facing side. They found warmer weather further south in Baja California Sur, where they arrived just in time for gray-whale migration season and stayed on for six months. At Cabo Pulmo's marine park near the southern tip of the peninsula, young Lennox, the family's little Aquaman, encountered mobula rays, whales, sea lions, and dolphins during his underwater excursions, deepening his love and respect for the ocean.

As spring turned to summer, the family found the temperatures on the peninsula increasingly difficult, so they crossed over to mainland Mexico, where they found lush tropical vegetation and shocking, 100-percent humidity. Traveling through the major cities of Mazatlán and Guadalajara, the adventurers reached the former silver-mining town of Guanajuato, where they were invited to participate in a traditional *temazcal* ceremony. A Nahuatl word meaning "house of steam," *temazcal* is a traditional ceremony performed for spiritual cleansing and physical detoxification—the bath's steam is created when water is poured over hot, volcanic rocks.

They found welcome respite from the heat in the ancient Mesoamerican city of Teotihuacan (7,540 feet/ 2,298 meters above sea level), an archeological site near Mexico City famous for its two sibling pyramids: the Pyramid of the Sun and the Pyramid of the Moon. In the nearby La Malinche National Park (named for the Nahua woman who acted as Cortés's translator), they climbed the dormant peak of the mountain bearing the same name, which reaches a dizzying height of 14,639 feet (4,462 meters). If it hadn't been so foggy at the summit, they would have been treated to breathtaking views over the Trans-Mexican Volcanic Belt.

The Chiapas town of San Cristóbal de Las Casas—with its mild highland temperatures, gorgeous light, and stunningly well-preserved colonial architecture—captivated Leander, Maria, and Lennox, and they stayed for several days. Back at sea level, they found relief in the many *cenotes* scattered throughout Mexico. These karst caves, filled with crystal-clear fresh water and often tucked away in the hinterlands, offered refreshing oases.

Soon it was time for a brief trip across the border into Guatemala, to extend the family's Mexican visas. They sensed that the end of their epic trip was drawing near, but needed a bit more time to be sure. Their experience of living on the road for seven years had been an extraordinary adventure, one that had transformed all of them. There had been many unforgettable experiences; they had also faced numerous challenges, from bureaucratic requirements to countless repairs—all alongside a growing teenager with changing needs. This particular style of mobile lifestyle had become very popular since the emergence of Covid-19, but it no longer felt right for the family. It was time to find new paths. The thought that the journey might soon end gave them all a queasy feeling, but the trio couldn't decide whether this was a good or bad sign. Yet they pushed forward with their plan. With the help of their shipping agent, they booked a freighter for Akela, which would carry the truck from Brunswick, Georgia—just north of Florida in the United States—across the Atlantic to Belgium. With this shipping slot booked, they set their final deadline.

The port of Brunswick was 2,175 miles (3,500 kilometers) from their current location, and the ship was scheduled to depart in a month. With these parameters set, the final section of the route led them north along the Gulf of Mexico, then through the U.S. states of Texas, Louisiana, Mississippi, Alabama, and Florida. The temperatures remained scorching hot, turning Akela into an oven-on-wheels. They spent most nights of this section of their journey in noisy Walmarts or gas-station parking lots. Luckily, Florida is a state renowned for its numerous natural springs, some of the largest and most beautiful in the world. Ichetucknee was one of these, and here, the family enjoyed a few relaxed days beside crystal-clear waters, preparing for the journey home and looking back over the highlights of the last two years. There were many: the long chain of the Rocky Mountains, the vast plains of Canada, freshwater lakes in Alberta, the deserts of California and Mexico, and the variety of animals—from bears, wolves, and bison to snakes, lizards, and birds—not to mention the extraordinary marine life they encountered. Each season had revealed different facets of the landscape, unfurling a kaleidoscope of colors that had captivated the hearts of the three adventurers.

Upon arriving in the small town of Brunswick, the family rented a motel near the port and used the remaining days to prepare Akela for shipping. The big day quickly approached. Once Akela was parked and ready for departure at the port, the family set off for the airport to fly back to Europe. A couple of weeks later, they were all reunited on European soil.

CANADA

# Going West: Getting Back to Basics in Alberta and British Columbia

Deep valleys, glittering glaciers, and clear mountain lakes at the head of the Rockies

They spent their days on challenging mountain hikes, enjoying icy dips in glacier lakes and warming themselves by campfires at secluded campsites.

CANADA

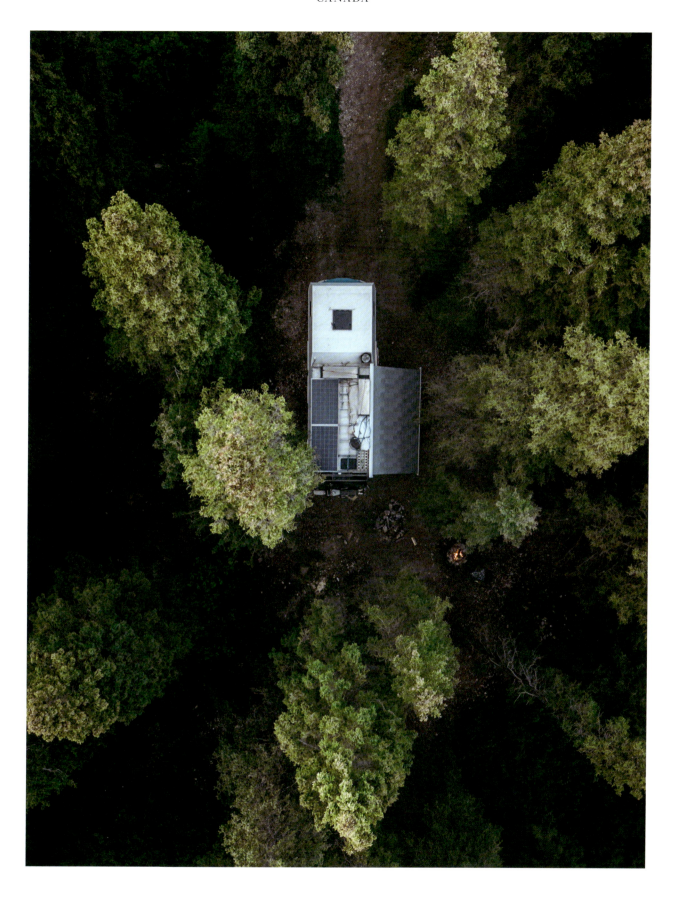

Akela, well hidden at a secluded campsite in the Ghost River Wilderness Area (above), found in the rugged Canadian Rockies (opposite).

Varying light conditions beautifully highlight a small waterfall on a hike through a forest in Alberta (opposite). A relatively common gray-breasted woodpecker, searching for food beneath a tree's peeling bark (above).

CANADA

## *Monuments to Cultural Heritage*

---

Totem poles, like these at Alert Bay on Cormorant Island, are significant cultural and historical symbols for the Indigenous peoples of Canada's Pacific Coast. These totem poles can depict myths, legends, and important community events, as well as the social status and power of a family or clan. Alert Bay is also home to the world's tallest totem pole, which stands an impressive 173 feet (53 meters) in height (above).

The annual salmon migration provides a feast not just for the bears, but for eagles and otters—the area's entire ecosystem relies on the abundant feast provided by the salmon run.

A salmon returns to its birthplace after weeks of upstream travel, ready to spawn (above right). After fulfilling their difficult mission, many fish die from sheer exhaustion. The snow-capped peaks of the Rocky Mountains tower above the icy, wooded valley (opposite).

Amid the rugged Rocky Mountains, with their deep valleys, glittering glaciers, and clear lakes, the three began to feel at home once more.

USA

# Face to Face with Awe-Inspiring Natural Wonders

Majestic mountains and Wild West scenery
in the spiritual home of the road trip

USA

## A Monument of Time and Mysteries

---

Once home to the Ancestral Puebloan peoples and a place of deep and continued significance to several Native American tribes, the Grand Canyon offers visitors dramatic lessons in human and geological history. At both sunrise and sunset in the Grand Canyon, the interplay of light and shadow makes for spectacular views (opposite).

While in Montana, between the Grand Tetons and Glacier National Park, Leander, Lennox, and Maria had an unforgettable encounter with a mother grizzly bear and her four lively cubs. From a safe distance, the three watched as the bear guided her cubs safely through the forest, imparting crucial survival skills to her young. The scene left a lasting impression on the observers (above).

After a seamless customs clearance, the adventure in
the land of unlimited possibilities could begin.

---

North America sometimes gives the impression of encompassing the diversity of all the world's continents.
Here one finds not just the fertile plains of a place like Wyoming, with its lush meadows and dense forests (opposite), but also
the landscape of a place like Joshua Tree National Park, with its sun-bleached scrub and distinctive Joshua trees (above).

Another stunning example of North America's diversity: a rugged and sharply towering mountain range in Idaho that thrilled the family's climbing hearts (opposite). The spiritual site of Sedona, a city in Arizona renowned for its red rock formations and energy vortexes (above).

MEXICO

# From the Baja Peninsula to the End of the Road

Mesoamerican pyramids, migrating gray whales, and silver mining towns en route to journey's end

*Temazcal* is a traditional ceremony performed for spiritual cleansing and physical detoxification—the bath's steam is created when water is poured over hot, volcanic rocks.

Baja California in Mexico is renowned not only for its diverse underwater world (opposite), but also its deep-rooted spiritual traditions, such as the *temazcal* steam-bath ritual (above left).

MEXICO

A majestic gray whale off the western coast
of Baja California Sur (above). Lennox freediving
in a mystical cenote in Mexico (opposite).

## Chasing Waterfalls

---

The adventurous trio was fortunate to visit the El Chiflón waterfall in Chiapas, Mexico, just before the rainy season that turns the shimmering turquoise water to a muddy, raging stream. Hidden deep in the rainforest, the waterfall cascades over multiple tiers, with the highest reaching approximately 390 feet (120 meters). The pools formed below invite swimming and exploration, much to Lennox's delight.

# The Adventuring Mindset

Embarking on a global 4WD touring adventure, a family set off on a journey that intertwined thrilling exploration with demanding responsibilities. Free from conventional rules and regulations, the long journey involved navigating thousands of miles of road and an endless variety of landscapes, not to mention numerous challenges, from encounters with wildlife and cultural differences to breakdowns and bureaucratic hurdles. It is a unique way of life that demands self-reliance and informed decision-making.

Throughout their travels, the family witnessed the planet's stunning beauty, as well as its vulnerability, gaining a profound insight into the number and variety of environmental and social issues affecting our delicate and interconnected ecosystems.

Leander and Maria's son and constant companion Lennox developed a passion for marine life, especially whales and dolphins, inspiring the family to focus their work on ocean conservation. They believe strongly in the importance of teaching younger generations about environmental stewardship to shape a sustainable future. As storytellers, Leander and Maria use their adventure to both entertain and educate, raising global awareness about critical issues. Committed to sustainable living, they are dedicated to supporting environmental causes and nurturing a conscious mindset in their son, striving to live independently while fostering a deeper connection with nature.

# Life on the Road

*Around the World on Four Wheels*

This book was conceived, edited, and designed by gestalten.

Written by Maria Zehentner
Photography by Leander Nardin

Edited by Robert Klanten and Laura Allsop

Contributing editors: Maria Zehentner and Leander Nardin
akela.world/@akela.world

Editorial Management by Anna Diekmann

Design and layout by Stefan Morgner
Map design by Greg Franco/lecartographiste.com

Photo Editor: Madeline Dudley-Yates

Typeface: Magneta by Neil Summerour

Printed by aprinta druck GmbH, Wemding
Made in Germany

Published by gestalten, Berlin 2025
ISBN 978-3-96704-171-2

© Die Gestalten Verlag GmbH & Co. KG, Berlin 2025

All rights reserved. No part of this publication may be reproduced or transmitted in any form or by any means, electronic or mechanical, including photocopy or any storage and retrieval system, without permission in writing from the publisher.

Respect copyrights, encourage creativity!

For more information, and to order books, please visit www.gestalten.com

Bibliographic information published by the Deutsche Nationalbibliothek.
The Deutsche Nationalbibliothek lists this publication in the Deutsche Nationalbibliografie; detailed bibliographic data is available online at www.dnb.de

This book was printed on paper certified according to the standards of the FSC®.

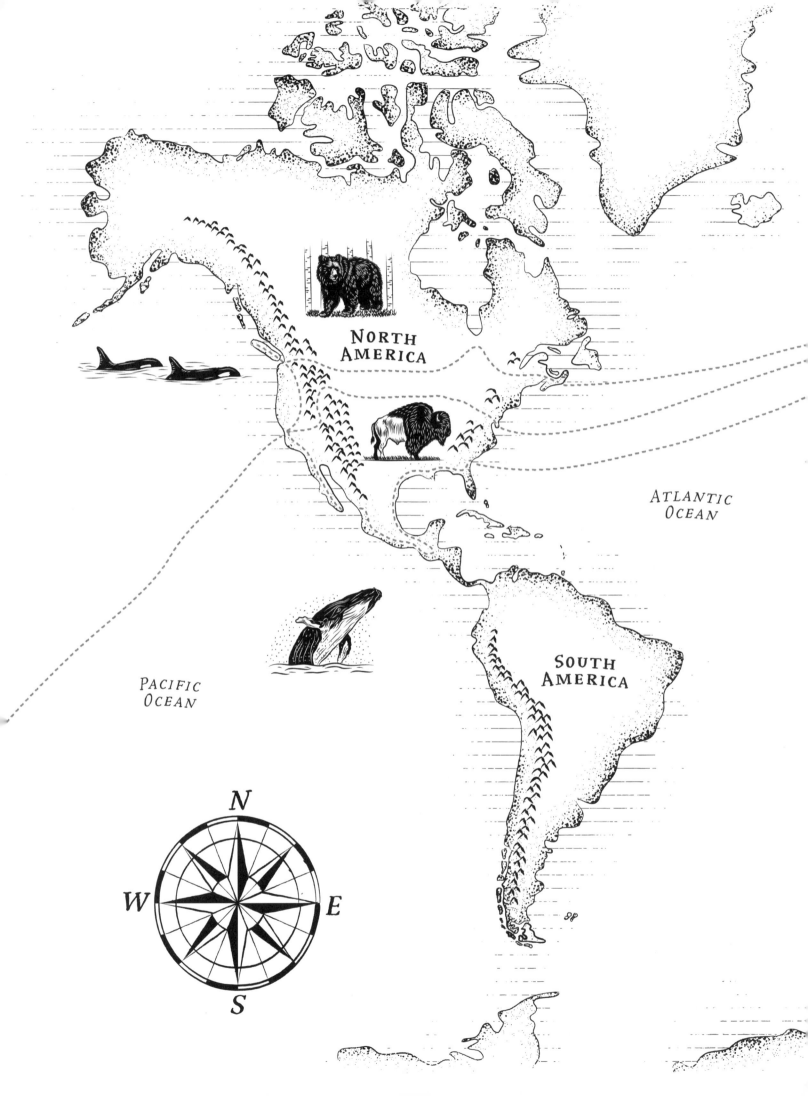